डॉ. किरण बेदी

नेतृत्वनिर्मिती

पोलीस जीवनातील संस्मरणीय प्रसंगांचे सचित्र दर्शन

अनुवाद: सुप्रिया वकील

मेहता पब्लिशिंग हाऊस

Please contact us at **Mehta Publishing House Pvt. Ltd.**
✆ +91 020-24476924 / 24460313 / Mob. No. 9545000513
Email : production@mehtapublishinghouse.com
Website : www.mehtapublishinghouse.com
◆ या पुस्तकातील लेखकाची मते, घटना, वर्णने ही त्या लेखकाची असून त्याच्याशी प्रकाशक सहमत असतीलच असे नाही.

CREATING LEADERSHIP by **Dr. KIRAN BEDI**

Translated into Marathi Language by **Supriya Vakil**

नेतृत्वनिर्मिती / कुमारसाहित्य
लेखक : डॉ. किरण बेदी
अनुवाद : सुप्रिया वकील
author@mehtapublishinghouse.com
मराठी अनुवादाचे व प्रकाशनाचे हक्क : मेहता पब्लिशिंग हाऊस प्रा. लि.

संस्थापक : सुनील मेहता
प्रकाशक : मेहता पब्लिशिंग हाऊस. प्रा लि.,
१९४१, सदाशिव पेठ, माडीवाले कॉलनी, पुणे ३०.
✆ ०२०-२४४७६९२४

मुखपृष्ठ व आतील चित्रे : श्री. प्रभात श्रीवास्तव
मुद्रक : श्री मुद्रा.
प्रथमावृत्ती : डिसेंबर, २०२२
किंमत : ₹ २५०/-
P BOOK ISBN 9789394258037

अर्पणपत्रिका

माझे आईवडील, प्रेम व प्रकाश पेशावरिया यांच्यासोबत मी.

''बेटा, कायम लक्षात ठेव- आयुष्य उतारासारखं असते, त्यात तुम्ही वर तरी चढता नाहीतर खाली तरी जाता.''

''पापा, हे मी कधीही विसरलेली नाही. मी माझे काम थांबवून विसावलेली नाही. मी स्वत:साठी कामे निर्माण करतीय.''

''पापा, हे सचित्र दर्शन तुम्ही वरून पाहात असाल अशी मला आशा आहे.''

''किरण, मोठी हो, ते इतरांना देण्यासाठी.''

''मम्मा, मी रोज सकाळी उठते ती स्वत:ला ऊर्जा देण्यासाठी, ज्यामुळे मी इतरांना काही देण्यायोग्य बनू शकेन. तू आयुष्यभर जो जीवनमार्ग अनुसरलास, त्याच पाऊलखुणा मी गिरवते आहे.''

''मम्मी, तूही डॅडींसोबत वरून हे सचित्र दर्शन पाहाशील अशी मला आशा आहे.... कारण हे सगळे तुझ्याविना शक्यच नव्हते.''

''पप्पा आणि मम्मा, मला तुमची रोज आठवण होते...''

भारतीय पोलीस सेवेतील पहिल्या महिलेने काय केले व कसे केले हे
भावी पिढ्यांना कळावे यासाठी हा लेखनप्रपंच... आणि एका मुलीला
उच्चपदावरील पोलीस अधिकारी बनवण्यात तिच्या आईवडिलांची भूमिका
किती महत्त्वपूर्ण असते ही गोष्ट कळण्यासाठीसुद्धा.

माझे सर्व प्रशिक्षक, शिक्षक, वरिष्ठ, गुरू, समर्थक, कुटुंबीय, मित्रपरिवार
व सहकारी.... तुमच्यामुळे हे शक्य झाले!

'मेकिंग ऑफ द टॉप कॉप मधून....

१९७५ सालच्या प्रजासत्ताक दिन संचलनात दिल्ली पोलीस दलाचे नेतृत्व करताना

संचलनानंतर माझ्या आईसोबत

INDIA TODAY November 16–30, 1978 Rs 3.50
The Fortnightly Newsmagazine

Images India Pictures by KISHORE CHAND—National Herald

WOMEN have traditionally been dubbed the weaker sex. But 29-year-old Kiran Bedi, Deputy Commissioner of Police in the personnel department at police headquarters in Delhi, can outsmart any man.

Refusing to be intimidated by angry Sikhs brandishing kirpans and lathis, she led her men into straight pitched battles with the demonstrators and fought more bravely than many of her male counterparts. Injuries on her leg and elbow did not deter her as she charged again and again to keep the Akalis at bay.

Married to an Amritsar businessman, Bedi is a mother of a three-year-old girl, she joined the Indian Police Service in 1972. Throughout her childhood, she was encouraged by her parents to be independent, resolute and tough. Her love for outdoor activities got her interested in tennis. She spent a considerable amount of her energy on tennis courts, playing several tournaments and eventually winning the Asian Women's Championship. From the active and energetic life as a tennis champion, she switched over and became a policewoman.

For Bedi crowd control is a challenge like many others she has faced in her life. very important part in such a situation."

When Akali demonstrators, protesting against the Nirankari Samagam turned violent on November 5 and threatened to break through the police cordon at India Gate, it was Bedi who rallied the demoralized police force around and controlled the mob.

अकाली-निरंकारी आंदोलन अशा भयंकर वळणावर येऊन ठेपले होते की, नंग्या तलवारी नाचवणारे आंदोलक पाहून सगळे पुरुष पोलीस पळून गेले होते आणि मी एकटीच उरले होते.... मला आत्मरक्षण करावे लागणार होते... माझे मलाच. त्या वेळी मला क्रीडा प्रशिक्षण, शारीरिक ताकद आणि खंबीर कणखरपणा उपयोगी पडला. या आंदोलनादरम्यान शौर्याने कर्तव्य बजावल्याबद्दल मला पोलीस सेवेतील माझ्या अवघ्या तीन वर्षांच्या कालवधीत पोलीस शौर्य पदक (मेडल फॉर गॅलन्ट्री) मिळाले.

शिकवण: बालपणी आत्मसात केलेले नेतृत्वगुण आपल्याला मोठेपणी खूप उपयोगी पडतात. म्हणून हे गुण आत्मसात करायला लवकर सुरुवात करा.

"Jai Jawahar -" NEW Delhi-8- I APRIL 1980

• न सोती है ..... न सोने देती है _ वेस्ट दिल्ली की पुलिस,

डिप्टी कमिश्नर किरन बेदी।

जिस दिन से श्रीमती किरन बेदी ने डिप्टी कमिशनर पुलिस वेस्ट दिल्ली ज़िला के पद का भार संभाला है एक दिन भी पूरी रात को वह न आप सोई हैं और न ही अपने किसी मातहत को सोने दिया है, हर रात चाहे वह काली रात हो चाहे चांदनी _ आपकी गाड़ी का चक्का घूमता फिरता रहता है, हर रात हर तरफ गश्त होती रहती है, गश्त नाकाबंदी, जनता की सेवा, और नगरिकों के जान व माल की रक्षा के लिये सब मातहतों को इलाका में ही डिय़ूटी पर सरगरम रखती हैं। 11 बजे रात आप मोती नगर कीरती नगर की सड़कों पर घूम रही होती हैं तो बारह बजे शकूर बस्ती, नांगलोई में सीटी बजा रही नज़र आती हैं एक बजे नजफगढ़ के बाज़ारों में घूमने वाली किरन बेदी 2 बजे रात जिस समय सारी दुनिया मज़े की नींद सो रही होती है जनकपुरी के इलाका की गश्त कर रही होती है, मादीपुर, शकूरपुर, पीतमपुरा, राजोरी गार्डन हर जगह रात को गश्त और कड़ी चैकिंग के बाद सुबह 10 बजे फिर अपने आफिस में काम करती नज़र आती हैं मोतीनगर, राजोरी गार्डन, पंजाबी बाग, नांगलोई, नजफगढ़, जनकपुरी तिलक नगर इलाकों के किसी

Joint night patrolling

By A Staff Reporter

NEW DELHI, February 8.

THE place — a street in a small residential colony of West Delhi. Time — a little after midnight. Suddenly the silence of the night is broken by the tap of police boots as a patrolling party moves along, checking doors and examining suspicious-looking shadows caused by erratic street lights. As the party approaches closer, one sees about half a dozen policemen, snug in their great coats, month ago, immediately after Mrs Kiran Bedi, the first woman Indian police officer, took over as deputy commissioner of police in the West District.

Mrs Bedi took charge of the district at a time when the people of the area were in a state of panic over a spate of armed robberies and dacoities. Faced with the twin task of curbing the incidence of crime and restoring the people's confidence, Mrs Bedi went about it with the instinct of a woman.

by citizens, police

were also put up at vantage points in the district. The officers, especially

night patrolling in their areas. Mrs Bedi, who declined to take credit for

सत्तास्थाने तुम्हाला इतरांच्या अधिकाधिक भल्यासाठी साधनस्रोत निर्माण करण्याचे सामर्थ्य बहाल करतात. जेव्हा आम्हाला रात्री गस्त घालण्यासाठी मनुष्यबळ कमी पडत होते तेव्हा आम्ही स्थानिक कल्याण संस्थांद्वारे रात्रसुरक्षा रक्षकांची व्यवस्था केली आणि ग्रामीण युवकांना स्वयंस्फूर्तीने या कार्यात सहभागी होण्यासाठी प्रेरित केले. लवकरच आम्हाला गस्त घालण्यासाठी पुरेसे मनुष्यबळ मिळाले. परिणामी रात्रीच्या गुन्ह्यांत लक्षणीय कपात झाली आणि लोकांना दिलासा मिळाला. पोलिसांसोबत अशा सुरक्षा-सहभागाचे अपेक्षित फळ मिळाले.

शिकवण: तुम्ही ज्या लोकांची सेवा करता, त्या लोकांना समस्यांतून मार्ग निघायला हवे असतात, त्यांना सबबी नको असतात. त्यांच्या समस्या सोडवा.

INDIA TODAY

June 1–15, 1981, Rs 4.00

BEAT BOX

A Popular Move

IN sharp contrast to the bruised and battered image that plagues the police force in most parts of the country, the police of Delhi's populous West District have of late been consciously turning out in their Sunday best, as it were, and wooing the public in a way that, with encouragement, could become a trend-setting move in cooperative peace-keeping.

Kicking off with a widely attended oath-taking ceremony on New Year's Day in which the entire staff of the West District police swore "to help anybody in need", this year alone more than 100 open-house public meetings have been held to encourage a dialogue with the community and to evolve effective methods of law enforcement ...

... deal now."

But the most important result of this system is the policeman's debut in the civic arena, as an arbiter and peace counsellor. Of the more than 800 complaints that are processed by the beat box constables every day, several are of a nature that would draw a blank at the police station.

Community members often seek out the beat box constable to settle petty disputes between squabbling couples or neighbourhood brawlers. As constable Rameshwar Dayal of Mongolpuri resettlement area said: "I have been sorting out all sorts of problems—husband-and-wife problems, drunkards, women squabbling at the water queues and so on. We are like a *sarpanch* in a village and people treat us like that."

The beat box system seems to have paid off with a major psychological coup for the ... role as a community leader with the full backing of the neighbourhood, serves not only to motivate him but also does wonders for his sagging self-esteem.

Clean Home: Said Kiran Bedi, the dapper, rakish, deputy commissioner of police, West District, and the moving force behind the experiment in cooperative peace-keeping: "Who would not accept a policeman who is ready to help? I would, if I were a citizen." With a woman's home-making instincts Bedi has set about putting her house in order, with a zeal that brooks no barriers. "The beat constable has started thinking that the beat is his home. Just as his home has to be kept clean, so has his beat to be kept clean," said Bedi.

Behind the zeal is a conviction that any social scientist will share—that combating crime and keeping the peace is an activity which involves the entire community, and the police can only be effective so long as they enjoy the support and cooperation of the community. By making public relations the bedrock of peace-keeping and law enforcement, Bedi has scored where strong-arm methods have failed. But support is slowly gathering. Says P.S. Bhinder, the embattled ...

राजौरी गार्डन में पुलिस बूथ बनाये गये हैं

–कार्यालय संवाददाता–

नयी दिल्ली, ३ फर. रौजडेन्ट
फेयर एसोसियेशन, राज
र्डन ने असामाजिक तत्वों
लाफ कारगर कार्रवाई कर
रि पुलिस तथा जनता के बी
हार्द्रपूर्ण सम्बन्ध बनाने के लि
क योजना बनायी है.

इस योजना के अन्तर्गत राज
ार्डन में दो पुलिस बूथ बन
ये हैं. इन बूथों के निर्माण
ाने वाला तमाम खर्च राज
ार्डन निवासियों ने वहन कि
है.

इन बूथों का उद्घाटन पश्
दिल्ली पुलिस उपायुक्त श्रीम
करण बेदी आज सायं करेंगी.

इन बूथों में दिन-रात पु

3 More 'Beat Boxes' In West Delhi

By A Staff Reporter

Three more "beat boxes" were installed by the police on Wednesday in West Delhi, to improve co-ordination with the people.

The beat boxes, which are to be manned by constables on the beat in the particular area, were opened in Mukherjee Park, Chowkhandi and Ganesh Nagar.

A Press release by the police said the people of Chowkhandi and Mukherjee Park had promised to provide telephones at the beat boxes in their areas

Punjab police for beat box system

NEW DELHI, Aug 3 (PTI).

Impressed by the beat box system in West Delhi, the Punjab police have sent an officer here to study it for adoption in the state.

Mr R. P. Joshi, senior superintendent of police, Faridkot, went round the west district on Sunday and discussed with a cross-section of the people and beat constables the working of the system.

He told the station house officer, Tilak Nagar, that the beat box system was revolutionary.

A beat box system was recently introduced in Bhatinda.

सुनिश्चित प्रतिसाद देत तुमच्या दारापर्यंत पोहोचणे हे पोलीस सेवेचे योग्य रूप होय. 'पोलीस बीट बॉक्स' या नव्या प्रकारच्या व्यवस्थेद्वारे आम्ही ते साध्य केले. या व्यवस्थेनुसार त्या-त्या भागाचा पोलीस अधिकारी - म्हणजेच 'बीट ऑफिसर' त्या भागातील वस्तीच्या केंद्रस्थानी नियुक्त करण्यात आल्यामुळे त्या भागातील नागरिकांना त्याच्यापर्यंत पोहोचणे सहजसुलभ झाले व तत्पर कारवाईची सोय झाली. या 'बीट बॉक्सेस'साठी स्थानिक लोकांचे योगदान लाभले.

शिकवण: तुम्ही तुमच्या सामान्य कार्यांची पूर्तता कशा प्रकारे करता यावरून तुमच्या नेतृत्वकौशल्याची परीक्षा होते.

BOOTLEGGERS OFF KEEL IN WEST POLICE DISTT.

PATRIOT, 11 APR 1980

Our Staff Reporter

IN Delhi's West police district the word is out: No future in bootlegging. Hundreds of Sansi tribe people, who in the past had made their living selling countrymade liquor 'imported' from neighbouring States, are now clamouring for regular employment.

The change has come because of the relentless drive by west district police chief Kiran Bedi to root out the liquor traffic. In the past three months alone, 302 persons have been arrested, among them 138 women.

The change in the mood of the Sansis was evident at a meeting organised in Madipur a few days ago with Mrs Bedi. One by one the Sansis stood up to plead that they be given bank loans to set-up cottage industries and allowed community facilities so that they can get back on the rails.

Chinto a middle aged woman with 10 children, begged "I have sold illicit liquor all my life—at least two bottles a day. But now I have no means to support my children and my husband is ill. Please find me some work."

There were others who spoke in the same vein. A man who hailed from Sialkot said he had been earning

demands for rehabilitation. Mrs Bedi made it clear to them that the police would brook no denial in curbing their nefarious practices but could offer them no alternative source of work. The rest, she said, was up to them.

Police records show that there
are 935 known bootle
cluding 222 women, in
With some still unkno
gure could go higher.
to manufacture liquor
own stills, but after
been unearthed they
stuff for the wholesa
drive in their cars f
the border. A motor
cedes the car carryi
quor in tyres or bot
the night and if the
clear, the stuff is
a prearranged spot to
up later. The lack of
by State polices has
the flushing out of
salers and the local
pretty much left on
Meanwhile the liquo
way into the mouth
toughs and from the
tale of petty theft, sta
other crimes emanate.
cutting down of the s
whole crime pattern
trict may change and
of the dozens of chil
are the only ones who

National Herald 12/9/81

Directory of west distt criminals

By Our Staff Reporter

NEW DELHI, July 11—The west district police have brought

"Ready reckoner" of criminals

NEW DELHI, July 11 (P.T.I.) — Now a "ready reckoner" of criminals of West Delhi has been brought out.

Mrs Bedi said that copies of the manual would be supplied to all the nine police stations in the district. This would enable the duty officer to immediately check the antecedents of criminals brought to the police station.

At present, Mrs Bedi said, the duty officer of a police station had to consult at least 18 registers to check the antecedents of a criminal.

The district presently maintained a crime record office work of which would be further streamlined and facilitated with the publication of the manual of criminals.

Tribune - 12/9/81

Policemen serve tea to ex-criminals

By A Staff Reporter

On the eve of Diwali on Sunday the West Delhi policemen invited over 350 people who are believed to have left the life of crime, to tea in nine police stations of the area.

The district's outgoing Deputy Commissioner of Police, Mrs Kiran Bedi, said in the police records these people were bad characters but were reported to have left the

Criminals on the mend entertained

NEW DELHI, Oct 26 (PTI).

East Delhi police, on Sunday, organised a unique Diwali-eve celebration.

More than 350 persons, entered in police records as bad characters and with externment proceedings against them, but believed to have left the life of crime, were entertained to tea by policemen at the nine police stations of the district, the outgoing DCP, Mrs Kiran Bedi, said today.

She said that the 360 former criminals vowed not to take to crime again. The police also assured them that they would not be harassed. The guests in turn promised to give information about criminals in the area to the police.

Mrs Bedi said that as on every Diwali eve, the policemen and officers in the district have been

दिल्लीच्या पश्चिम जिल्ह्यात काम करत असताना, गुन्ह्यांची पुनरावृत्ती कमी करण्यासाठी प्रत्येक गुन्हेगाराला सुधारण्यासाठी संधी देणे हे आमचे सुस्पष्ट धोरण होते. आम्ही बीट पोलीस ऑफिसर्सना नोंदवह्या दिल्या होत्या. पोलीस ठाण्यात आम्ही पूर्वीच्या सराईत हातभट्टीवाल्यांना चहापाण्याला बोलवायचो. अशा शेकडो जणांच्या नोंदी त्या वहीत केल्या जात असत व त्यांच्या सामाजिक पुनर्वसनाची नोंदही त्यात केली जात असे. त्यामुळे या लोकांना सामाजिक स्वीकृती लाभण्यासही साहाय्य होत असे.

शिकवण: लोक गैरमार्गाला लागू शकतात, पण त्यांना सुधारण्याची संधी दिली तर ते सुधारू शकतात ही गोष्ट नेता जाणतो.

अब पुलिस की निगाह स्कूली बच्चों पर पड़ी है

– सान्ध्य टाइम्स संवाददाता –

नयी दिल्ली, १३ अक्तूबर. पश्चिमी दिल्ली पुलिस ने पिछले १५ दिनों के दौरान स्कूल नहीं जाने वाले बच्चों की व्यापक जांच का अभियान चलाया.

उपायुक्त श्रीमती किरण बेदी के अनुसार इस दौरान ४५९ बच्चों की जांच की गयी. वीर कान्सटेबलों की मदद से की गयी इस व्यापक जांच के दौरान १७५ ऐसे बच्चों का पता लगाया गया, जो किसी न किसी कारण से स्कूल नहीं जाते थे. पुलिस ने इन बच्चों को पुनः उनके स्कूलों में भरती करवाया.

पुलिस ने इस दौरान नियमित रूप से स्कूल नहीं पहुंचने वाले बच्चों का भी पता लगाया. ये बच्चे घर से स्कूल जाने के लिए रवाना होते थे लेकिन बजाय स्कूल जाने के, रास्ते में कंचे, ताश और गुल्ली-डंडा खेलते रहते थे.

पुलिस ने इन बच्चों के माता-पिता से सम्पर्क किया और बच्चों को नियमित रूप से स्कूल पहुंचाने की व्यवस्था की गयी.

५० के करीब ऐसे बच्चे थे, जिन्हें विभिन्न कारणों से स्कूलों से निकाल दिया गया था. पुलिस ने स्वयं हस्तक्षेप करके इन बच्चों को स्कूलों में फिर से दाखिल करवाया.

इन बच्चों के माता - पिता से अनुरोध किया गया है कि वे अपने बच्चों पर निगाह रखें.

इसके अलावा करीब ८० बच्चों को छोटा - मोटा काम दिलाया गया जिससे उनकी आमदनी का जरिया बन सके. क्योंकि ये बच्चे माता - पिता द्वारा पढ़ाई का खर्च नहीं दिये जाने के कारण, स्कूल नहीं जाते थे.

Sandhya Times :- August - 3

पुलिस अंकल ने बच्चों के साथ खेलना शुरू कर दिया

–सान्ध्य टाइम्स संवाददाता–

नयी दिल्ली, ३ अगस्त. "तुम अगर गंदा काम करोगे तो मैं पुलिस अंकल से शिकायत कर दूंगा."

छह-सात वर्षीय बच्चे ने परसों शाम अपने एक दोस्त से यह बात कही.

ये सारे बच्चे तिलकनगर पुलिस द्वारा चौखंडी में आयोजित किये गये खेलकूदों के दौरान इकट्ठे हुए थे.

पश्चिमी दिल्ली पुलिस ने बच्चों के मन से पुलिस का भय दूर करने और उनमें दोस्ती की भावना जगाने के लिए यह नया प्रयोग शुरू किया है.

इस कार्यक्रम के दौरान हर शनिवार को एक-एक वीर में वीर कांस्टेबल बच्चों के लिए खेलकूद आयोजित करेंगे. पुलिसवाले उनके साथ खेलेंगे. इन खेलों के दौरान अच्छा खेलने वालों को इनाम दिये जायेंगे.

"WE ARE PEACEFUL VILLAGERS NOW," SAY EX-CRIMINALS

SUN

Rs.3.25 VOL IV No.2 AUGUST 23,1980

SURPRISING BUT.. MEET THE POLICE MEN WHO HELP PEOPLE

There is Chandra Dutt, Anand Singh, Kartar Chand, Hardwari .and the list goes on. Such simple and decent names. And yet these people were once dreaded criminals in the villages around Delhi.

They not only used to commit crimes in their own areas but also shattered the peace of city life. Goondaism, pick-pocketing, dacoity and murder were rampant.

"This had to be stopped," says K.K. Chabra, Assistant Commissioner of Police, West District. "A system had to be evolved and the beat system was the best." Today all the villages of West District have beat constables who spend about eight hours on their beats. Each beat ... 8 to 9 villages. The ... visit the ... their ... have ... sys- ... opera- ... ordi- ... their ... aha ... nd ...

...nd created hell in the neighbour-...ood. Others stole parts of irriga-...on machines, destroyed crops, ...ought with lathis and even mur-...ered. But all this has stopped now. ...e are a peaceful village."

There is Jugti who himself nar-...ates his story, "I used to go to Ra-...asthan and bring 20 bottles of ...hara'. Each bottle cost me Rs. 2 ...nd I used to sell it for Rs. 10. So I ...s. 8 profit," he adds with a smile.

"But now I am only a farmer," he ...ays holding both his ears. "Madan...

WIFE-BEATING ENDS

"Crime is almost finished in Isapur," says Chandra Singh, who is a clerk in the Delhi Military Hospital. The village was notorious for its criminal activities

‘पोलीस बीट सिस्टीम’ ही प्राचीन व्यवस्था आहे, पण तिची अजिबातच अंमलबजावणी झाली नव्हती. या व्यवस्थेचे मूलतत्त्व म्हणजे त्या-त्या भागातील प्रत्येक बीट ऑफिसरवर त्या त्या भागाची संपूर्ण जबाबदारी सोपवणे. समाजाच्या गरजांनुसार निर्णय घेण्यासाठी आम्ही आमच्या पोलिसांच्या सबलीकरणाद्वारे ही व्यवस्था सुरू केली. या ‘कम्युनिटी पोलीस’ व्यवस्थेने नागरिकांची मने जिंकली आणि त्यातूनच ‘सामुदायिक स्वामित्व’ कल्पनेला बळ मिळाले.

शिकवण: सर्व संबंधितांचे सर्वंकष सबलीकरण घडवणे ही नेतृत्वाची परीक्षा असते. त्याचा सर्वंकष परिणाम घडला पाहिजे.

"Hold it, yaar... I think it's Kiran Bedi!"

The citizens of Delhi are presently witnessing a unique game of hide and seek between the car owners and the traffic police which is the outcome of a drive launched by Deputy Commissioner Police (traffic) Kiran Bedi against wrong parking. These days it is a common sight to see a car being dragged away by a police crane to the police station as a punishment for those who leave their vehicles parked at wrong places.

Considering the problem of wrong parking and traffic jams, it is a most welcome step taken by

SUNDAY

PM's car held

New Delhi: When the deputy police commissioner (traffic) Mrs Kiran Bedi started a drive against wrong parking last year, no one could have imagined that even the Prime Minister's car would come into the dragnet. But the impossible happened. On 5 August, when Mrs Gandhi and her family members were away in the USA, a traffic sub-inspector found a white Ambassador (DHI 1817), wrongly parked outside the Yusfzai Market, Connaught Circus, in the heart of the city. Only after he had made out a challan did he realise that it was the official car of the PM. The security men accompanying the car (which had gone there for repairs), pointed this out to the traffic officer ... was adamant. Wrong ... illegal, whether it be ... or a VIP, he told the ...

An enquiry has bee... the incident. As so... returned from her t... was brought to her n... of the enquiry is: how... of coordination be... security and the traf... Delhi police? Mrs ... however, made it ... question of putting ... officer who was ...

his duties did not arise. The incident, meanwhile has exposed a chink in the Delhi traffic police. The shop to which Mrs Gandhi's car went, Handa and Company, belongs to a friend of a powerful aide of the PM. The shop deals in car accessories and upholstery. The popularity of the shop attracts many carowners. But to take a car to the shop also invites a traffic challan because of the shop's location. The car park on the opposite pavement is usually overcrowed (as a popular restaurant and hotel are located there). The traffic police have been refusing to recognise the fact

that as long as Handa and Babbar Sons, two popular car accessory dealers, are located at the Yusufzai Mar-

View of the overcrowded parking space opposite Handa and Co

वाहतूक पोलीस व्यवस्थापनात, आम्ही बेताल वाहनचालकांना शिस्त लावण्यासाठी क्रेनच्या साहाय्याने वाहने उचलून नेऊ लागलो. या कामी आम्ही अविरत प्रयत्न करत होतो. यात आम्ही कुणालाही सोडले नाही, अगदी तत्कालीन पंतप्रधान श्रीमती इंदिरा गांधी यांची अधिकृत गाडीसुद्धा. यातून, कायदा सर्वांपेक्षा मोठा आहे हा स्पष्ट संदेश प्रसारित झाला. यामुळे रस्त्याचा वापर करणाऱ्या व्यक्तींचे वाहतूक पोलसांशी असणारे वर्तन रातोरात सुधारले.

शिकवण: नेतृत्व अडचणींना खंबीरपणे सामोरे जाते. ते कसल्याही दबावाला बळी पडत नाही.

Mrs Kiran Bedi, deputy commissioner, Delhi traffic police, talking to some of the auto-rickshaw drivers who got special awards at a function jointly organised by the Delhi traffic police and a leading tyre company at Inter-State Bus Terminus, Delhi, on Saturday.—TOI photo.

12 drivers honoured for honesty

By A Staff Reporter

NEW DELHI, June 26.

AUTO-RICKSHAW drivers in the Capital have the unenviable reputation of being extremely rude and often not so honest. They invariably overcharge passengers, refuse to take them to their destination if it does not suit them and react very sharply if the passengers dare challenge them. And for this they are always at the receiving end of brickbats and abuse from the general public.

But this is not always so. Twelve [illegible] including a taxi driver and a taxi driver who proved an exception [illegible] were felicitated at a spe[illegible] today, organised jointly [illegible] traffic police and a leading tyre company. The [illegible] was [illegible] police records [illegible] certificates and [illegible] certificates [illegible] of the men[illegible] tion of the men [illegible] in the last [illegible] as they marched proudly to the dais to receive their awards from Mrs Kiran Bedi, deputy commissioner of police, traffic. Kuldeep Singh Jaggi, one of the winners, proudly displayed his award. "It is good to know that at least somebody recognises the work done by us. Normally all we get is abuse from the people, he said. To Jaggi goes the credit of depositing with the police a purse containing cash and valuables left behind in his vehicle by a passenger.

Satinder Singh, another award-winner, returned 1,900 traveller cheques to the police left behind in his auto-rickshaw by an Australian tourist. Among the award-winners who got the loudest applause was taxi driver Narang Singh. There have been no complaints against him nor has he ever been challaned. In addition, he once returned a briefcase containing some important documents belonging to the personal assistant of the finance min[illegible] bag containing valuables and cash which were left behind in his taxi.

Speaking on the occasion, Mrs Bedi exhorted autorickshaw and taxi-drivers to be more polite and honest in their dealings with the passengers. She said although the situation had improved considerably, she still received innumerable letters from people complaining about the behaviour of autorickshaw drivers.

Mrs Bedi said the Delhi Traffic police had started maintaining records of both the good work done by the drivers and the complaints received against them.

She called for greater rapport between the drivers and the traffic police so that passengers were not put to any inconvenience. Mrs Bedi said her department had started giving lessons in road safety to drivers. The latter were also being coached about the traffic patterns during the coming Asian Games.

Mrs. Kiran Bedi, DCP (Traffic) helping a child ignite the torch to herald opening of the Children's Sports Evening in New Delhi on Saturday. — Herald photo

Children-cops bonanza ends

By Our Sports Reporter

NEW DELHI June 12 — The three-day sports bonanza, organised by the newly-formed Citizens—Delhi Traffic Police Coordination Committee, came to an end with hundreds of children, wearing a festive look, vying for honour in different sports events.

It was the first time a meet with a special aim to develo[illegible] sense amongst [illegible]

Mrs. Kiran Bedi, DCP (Traffic), talking to reporters said, judging from the overwhelming response that the meet has evoked, she has decided to organise such kind of children sports meet in different parts of the capital. The basic aim of organising such meets, According to Mrs. Bedi, was to eliminate the fear of police uniform amongst the children.

Watch out your headlights

Led by DCP Kiran Bedi, officers and men of the Delhi Traffic Police, armed with black paint and brushes, fanned out into the capital on Monday night painting ... create an awareness of the ... ards of dazzling headlights, ... traffic police appealed to mo... ists to get the top of their v... cles headlights painted black.

This is it!

By Sudhir Dar

Delhi cops paint vehicles' headlight

NEW DELHI, Apr. 27 (PTI): Led by D.C.P. Mrs Kiran Bedi, officers and men of the Delhi traffic police, armed with black paint and brushes, fanned out into the capital last night painting the upper half of the head... of 3000 four-wheeler ve...

The Statesman 4.5.82

Deadline to paint headlights over

By A Staff Reporter

Painting 16,000 vehicle headlights is about all that the Traffic Police could do. And while black is beautiful and the policemen, evidently, have enjoyed themselves with their brushes and cans of paint, the incubation period for motorists in Delhi is over. When they take their cars and other four-wheelers out on city roads on Tuesday without the headlights painted, they will be inviting a 50-rupee fine.

A spokesman of the Traffic Police said on Monday that prosecutions would begin at various points in the city on Tuesday. Following an amendment to the M... Vehicle Rules last year, blackening the upper portion of the headlight... been made compulsory.

While the Traffic Police ... stopped their free painting of headlights—a drive that has been on for the past week—there ...

दिल्लीतील रहदारी हा भयंकर प्रकार होता. वाहतूक पोलिसांना त्याबाबत कठोर कारवाईचे अधिकार नव्हते. आज आपण जे तंत्रज्ञान जाणतो, त्याचे अद्याप आपल्या देशात आगमन झाले नव्हते. पण नवव्या आशियायी क्रीडास्पर्धेसाठी शहर सुसज्ज असणे आवश्यक होते. त्यासाठी आम्ही नागरिकांना सहभागी करून घेऊन रस्ता सुरक्षा अभियान, पोलिसांचे कारवाईचे अधिकार वाढवणे, सार्वजनिक वाहतूक व्यवस्थेची सुरक्षा, प्रामाणिक वाहनचालकांना पुरस्कार अशासारख्या अनेक उपाययोजना केल्या.

शिकवण: जेव्हा तुमच्यावर असे काम सोपवले जाते, ज्यामध्ये बऱ्याच उणिवा आहेत, तेव्हा ते आव्हान म्हणून स्वीकारा आणि त्यामध्ये तुमच्या कौशल्याने काही वेगळे घडवून दाखवा.

DELHI TRAFFIC POLICE

introduce a motoring convenience for the

OPENING AND CLOSING CEREMONIES

Park and Ride Scheme

INDIAN EXPRESS, 13 NOV 1982

Games a

To tackle traffic complaints Delhi Traffic Police extend a helping hand.

Are you paying correct fares?

Do keep in mind the latest revised rates

Hindustan Times 21 NOV 1982

TAXI FARE CHART

[illegible]

AUTO RICKSHAW FARE CHART

Meter Reading	Fare Payable	Meter Reading	Fare Payable	Meter Reading	Fare Payable
[illegible]	[illegible]	[illegible]	[illegible]	[illegible]	[illegible]

Delhi Traffic Police lead the way to convenient General Parking for the Asian Games

P

Some do's and dont's for parking unlabelled vehicles:

Hindustan Times

Are you an Asian Games Ticket Holder? If Yes, Delhi Traffic Police answers your queries.

- How to reach the Stadia?
- About the various Road Diversions.
- Where to Park your Vehicle?
- About the Park and Ride Scheme.

at the Delhi Traffic Police Pavilion, Entry Gate No. 4, Pragati Maidan, New Delhi, from 1st November to 14th November 1982.

Hindustan Times

TIMES OF INDIA

Helicopter to hel

By A Staff Reporter

NEW DELHI, November 18.

SPECIALLY requisitioned Indian ir Force helicopter, in continu- wireless contact with the traffic ol room, will hover over the arlal Nehru Stadium and main in the vicinity to help regulate tomorrow on the opening day ations of the Asiad.

traffic police spokesman said Mathura Road, Ring Road, bindo Marg, Lal Bahadur Shas- larg, Panchsheel Marg and m Pitamah Marg will be kept constant monitoring.

police officer manning the heli- will advise the ground control any bottlenecks and the vol- of traffic on various roads to a smooth flow.

• • •

Indian Oil service station on

ciation has deci pulses out of De This would prices of pulses A six-man vigil been appointed implement its d

Under instruct ernment of Indi Municipal Corp 11 a.m. and clos ember 22 to De break shall be pass.

The existing o restored automa ber 6.

Second Saturd December fallin served as a full cember 3 shall in lieu thereof.

•

The first eve

grand success

BY
K.R. WADHWANEY
INDIAN EXPRESS, 5 DEC 1982

The first gold medal!

nations on their arrival in the capital.

Finally, a word about Indian sportsmen. A senior coach, associate with the Special Organising Committee (SOC), said "The organisers have taken little care of sportsmen and sweepers". There is sum and substance in this observation. A large number of sportsmen failed to receive than full compliment of uniforms and kit, while the sweepers were not provided any, although both worked harder than many senior SOC officials.

In the end, the greatest triumph was the way the traffic was kept moving during the Games, particularly on Saturday (closing ceremony) and the opening day (Nov 19). The police

egulate traffic

xport
Asiad.
the
ames.
has
on to
Gov-
the
en a
Nov

sal, arrangements have been made to carry the same number. For assemblage, eight EMU trains, 4 clockwise and 4 anti-clockwise, will run from Patel Nagar railway station to Sewa Nagar railway station between 12.50 and 14.25 hours. Similarly, at the time of dispersal, eight EMU trains, four in each direction, will leave

आशियायी क्रीडास्पर्धेदरम्यान वाहतूक व्यवस्थापनाची यशस्विता ही अथक योजना आखणे, साधनस्रोतांचे व्यवस्थापन, प्रशिक्षण आणि सिव्हिल सोसायटीचे योगदान या साऱ्याची फलनिष्पत्ती होती. राजकीय, प्रशासकीय व अंमलबजावणी करणाऱ्या यंत्रणांमध्ये, लहान-मोठ्या सर्व स्तरांमध्ये विलक्षण सुसूत्रता होती. संपूर्ण पोलीस दलाने सर्वशक्तीनिशी काम केले, परिणामी अभूतपूर्व यश मिळाले, ज्याची आजही आठवण काढली जाते.

शिकवण: जेव्हा एखादा नेता त्याच्या टीमवर विश्वास टाकतो, त्यांना अधिकार प्रदान करतो व त्यांना सबल करतो तेव्हा उद्दिष्टे साध्य होतातच.

CHOG-M: Another rehearsal on Nov. 20

By A Staff Reporter

PANJIM, Nov. 17: An overall rehearsal of arrangements for forth coming CHOG-M Retreat will be held on Nov 20. The Goa Traffic Police have declared the following diversions to be made on this day between 1 to 4 p.m.

Traffic from Panjim to Mapusa and vice-versa will be diverted via Betim and will be temporarily halted at O'Coqueiro.

Traffic from Margao and Vasco to Panjim will be diverted at Pilar-Neura-Old Goa road and regulated near Panjim bus stop according to the movement of the VVIP motorcade.

Traffic from Panjim to Margao or Vasco will follow the normal route and will be temporarily halted at Pato bridge according to the movement of the motorcade.

During the period of diversion the villages like Sta Cruz, Sirdao, Goa Velha, Pilar, Agassaim and Chicalim will be approachable from Panjim side only.

Traffic will also be temporarily halted at Chicalim intersection and Cortalim junction as per the movement of the motorcade.

Adequate number of wireless sets have been circulated by the Traffic Police to monitor the motorcade movement. Towing vehicles and ambulances have also been stationed at all strategic points.

Meanwhile the blue and white clad 900 NCC and NSS students of different colleges have also joined the police in the control of the traffic.

Mrs. Kiran Bedi, Superintendant of Police (Traffic) has expressed her satisfaction over the good enthusiasm shown by the student volunteers.

गोव्यामध्ये आमच्या लक्षात आले की, 'कॉमनवेल्थ हेडस् ऑफ गव्हर्मेंट' परिषदेसाठी येणाऱ्या व्हीआयपींच्या सुरक्षेच्यादृष्टीने, चाळीस किलोमीटर मार्गावर बंदोबस्तासाठी तैनात करायला पुरेसे वाहतूक पोलीस बळ नाही. मग आम्ही महाविद्यालयात शिकणाऱ्या मुला-मुलींशी संपर्क साधला. त्यांना रस्ता-सुरक्षेसंदर्भात प्रशिक्षित केले आणि या मुलांनी हे बंदोबस्ताचे काम केले. परत जाताना बऱ्याच व्हीआयपींनी त्यांचा ताफा थांबवून, गाडीतून उतरून या तरुण नागरिकांना धन्यवाद दिले. यामध्ये श्रीमती इंदिरा गांधीही होत्या.

शिकवण: तरुणाई हा सर्वात कमी उपयोगात येणारा साधनस्रोत आहे. त्यांना सहभागी करून घ्या. ही भविष्यासाठी सर्वोत्तम गुंतवणूक ठरेल.

IRON FOUNDRY
Ganj, Agra - 282004
Cable: Raj Foundry

Regd.No. D-(c)167 Vol LXIII No. 255

AIR SURCHARGE : Kathmandu: 25 paise; North-Eastern
Calcutta and beyond by rail: 15 paise;

Clash on Ramlila procession route

Sec. 144 in Walled City areas

HT Correspondent

NEW DELHI, Oct. 4 — Section 144 was imposed in Jama Masjid, Kotwali, Hauz Qazi and Town Hall police station areas of the Walled City this evening following clashes between the police and violent processionists who had wanted to take out a Ramlila procession through the traditional route and were refused permission.

Chandni Chow
Ajmeri Gate –
Maidan, where t
This route was
more than 100 y
Following the
Ramlila at the R
According to
puty Commissio
District), the D
had given an alt
processionists thr
Chowk and Dar
was communal t
of trouble if th
through the wall

Women in peace panels

Hindustan Times Correspondent

NEW DELHI, July 27 — The North District police has initiated a programme of women's participation in peace-

Police plan to maintain harmony

Express News Service

NEW DELHI, July 27

The North district police has started a programme of women's participation in peace-keeping and communal harmony.

Patriot 16.4.1988

Mrs Bedi and BJP

Mr Atal Behari Vajpayee is asking Mrs Kiran Bedi, IPS, recipient of the award of the President's police medal, to quit her post because while in all parts of the Capital except North Delhi, BJP agitators have been detained and let off, she arrested a number of them when they broke the police cordon in the north district and produced 18 of them before the magistrate. Mr Madan Lal Khurana, Mr Kedar Nath Sahni and other BJP councillors were forced to confess in the court that

महिलाओं के लिए एक विशेष प्रशिक्षण अभियान

Hindustan 27/7

(हमारे कार्यालय संवाददाता द्वारा)

नई दिल्ली, २७ जुलाई। उत्तरी जिला पुलिस ने महिलाओं के लिए एक विशेष प्रशिक्षण अभियान शुरू किया है।

महिलाओं को भी आगे आना चाहिए

श्रीमती बेदी ने बताया कि इस अभियान में उत्तरी जिले के अनेक वरिष्ठ अधिकारियों तथा सभी थानाध्यक्षों की पत्नियों को भी शामिल

एके दिवशी दिल्लीत मातब्बर राजकारणी मंडळींच्या नेतृत्वाखाली जबरदस्त आंदोलन झाले. मनाई आदेशाचा भंग केल्यामुळे सर्व प्रमुख नेत्यांना अटक झाली. त्यांनी गुन्हा कबूल केला, त्यांना दोषी ठरवण्यात आले. यातून अत्यंत ठळक संदेश मिळाला की सार्वजनिक सुरक्षेच्या संदर्भात तडजोड केली जाणार नाही. लवकरात लवकर, पुन्हा शांतता प्रस्थापित करण्यासाठी आम्ही महिला शांतता समिती स्थापन केल्या. त्यांनी पुन्हा सलोखा निर्माण करण्याचे अभूतपूर्व कार्य केले.

शिकवण: जे योग्य आहे ते करण्याबाबत कधीही तडजोड करू नका. कारण ते कार्य करणे हे तुमचे कर्तव्य आहे.

Agnihotri did write graffiti

Express News Service

NEW DELHI, April 19

Rajesh Agnihotri did write the obscene graffiti on the walls of the ladies' toilet in the Delhi university's botany department. This has been established by handwriting experts in the Central Forensic Science Laboratory (CFSL).

The CFSL report was "positive", the police said. The specimen handwriting sent to the lab and that on the walls of the toilet "matched", a senior police official said.

Rajesh Agnihotri was caught by students in the ladies' toilet of the department on April 4. He had been arrested once before in January for allegedly stealing the purse of a girl in St Stephen's College, once again from near the ladies' toilet. The arrest sparked off the lawyers' strike which was called off on Tuesday.

Mr Rajesh Kumar Agnihotri, the advocate whose handcuffing in January sparked off a nation-wide lawyers' strike, caught once again by girls and boys in Delhi University's botany department ladies toilet on Monday. Photo shows policemen questioning the lawyer who was arrested and released on bail later. — TOI photo by Sharad Saxena.

Women belonging to various organisations staging a demonstration near Boat Club on Friday to express solidarity with DCP (North) Kiran Bedi — Patriot photo.

Patriot SATURDAY, 13 FEBRUARY 1988

THE STATESMAN, FEBRUARY 13, 1988

A large number of women, including students, marched to the Home Minister's residence in New Delhi on Friday to express support for Mrs Kiran Bedi, Deputy Commissioner of Police. They presented a copy of a

प्रत्येक समाजात असे काही सामर्थ्यवान समूह असतात, जे स्वत:ला 'खास' समजत असतात. एकदा, कायद्याशी संबंधित व्यवसाय करणारी एक व्यक्ती चोरी करताना रंगेहाथ सापडली. पण त्या व्यक्तीची आपल्याला वेगळी वागणूक मिळावी अशी अपेक्षा होती. यातूनच पोलीस व त्या समूहातील काही सदस्य यांच्यात प्रदीर्घ कायदेशीर लढाई झाली. या लढाईत ना कुणी जिंकले ना हरले.

शिकवण: काही वेळा प्रवाहाविरुद्ध पोहण्याची मोठी किंमत चुकवावी लागते. ती किंमत चुकती करा.

THE HINDU
FRIDAY FEATURES-2

Removing darkness from the lives of addicts

Meditation exercise for the participants at the camp.

Clinic to reform criminals

THE HINDU 5-7-89

NEW DELHI

The North District Police intro 'cured' smack addicts to the Police ner, Mr. Ved Marwah, at a function What is most significant is that 69 of a criminal background. They were rehabilitated at a clinic being run at Mughal police post.

Clinic to reform criminals

THE HINDU 5-7-89

NEW DELHI, July 4.

The North District Police introduced 111 'cured' smack addicts to the Police Commissio-

De-addiction centre at police station

MID-DAY 4-7-89

ay. ve nd nra of lav go

By A Staff Reporter

In what is termed as a nove gesture in the annals of dru abuse, the guardians of th

areas like Najafgarh, Sl Mehrauli.

As a mark of apprecia

अपराधी सुधार योजना

—नगर संवाददाता—

नई दिल्ली, १४ फरवरी। उत्तर दिल्ली पुलिस उपायुक्त श्रीमती किरण बेदी की

कि इन स्कूलों से उन्हें पुलिस जनता सहयोग और अपराधियों के सुधार में काफी सफलता मिली है।

Reformatory schools for poor women

PATRIOT, 15 FEB,1987

Our Staff Reporter

"Reformatory schools" a project under which free training in sewing and knitting is given to women from the weaker sections has been launched recently by the Delhi Police along with a sewing machine firm.

Disclosing its objective on Saturday, DCP North Kiran Bedi and the company's national sales manager S Rajmani said that the purpose was to provide neglected and poor women training and education to enable them to earn

pany, Mr Rajmani said.

Mrs Bedi, on the other hand, on behalf of the Delhi Police, said the police would sponsor them for bank loans at concessional rates of interest, to enable them to set up their own self-employment facilities in terms of buying these machines and doing their own business.

The project also envisaged welfare scheme of free sewing and knitting training for the families of the police personnel to enable them to supplement the family income. There had been tremendous response from the women in the areas where the training project was set up, Mrs Bedi said.

The Hindu - 15-2-87

lice stations in areas where a high concentration of the economically backward people resided. Women from these selected groups will be provided free sewing and knitting education with the help of trained instructresses from the sewing machine

Scheme to make poor women self-employed

NEW DELHI, Feb. 14.

The Delhi police and the Indian Sewing Mach-

दारिद्र्य वंचितता, वाईट संगत आणि निरुद्देश जगणे यातून गुन्ह्यांचा जन्म होतो. आमच्या अधिकारक्षेत्रात येणाऱ्या झोपडपट्ट्या व बकाल वस्त्यांमध्ये हेच घडत होते. गुन्ह्यांची पुनरावृत्ती टाळण्यासाठी, आम्ही काही मूलभूत पावले उचलली आणि त्याच्या मूळ कारणावरच घाव घातला. यामध्ये आम्ही साक्षरता, अवैध दारू विक्रेत्या महिलांसाठी व्यवसाय कौशल्य प्रशिक्षण, व्यसनाधीन लोकांवर उपचार अशा उपक्रमांना प्रारंभ केला व हे सर्व 'नवज्योती इंडिया फाउंडेशन' या छत्राखाली एकत्र आणले.

शिकवण: तुम्ही तुमच्या नेतृत्वस्थानाचा उपयोग समस्यांच्या मूळाशी असणाऱ्या कारणांची उकल करण्यासाठी केला नाहीत, तर तुम्ही त्या स्थानास पात्र नाही.

PORTERS TO BE REGISTERED

THE STATEMAN, 11 JAN, 1987

By a Staff Reporter

Now if you see an overload
man in a parrot-green shirt, wi
a large number printed on t
back and an identity card witl
photograph pinned
will know that he
the traders in Ch
Lahori Gate, and
The business
these areas, appar
with the frequenc
the porters disappear with the
goods, have in collaboration wi
the Delhi Police, evolv
of registering

Being a good cop does reap rich dividends as constable Ranbir Singh of the Kingsway Camp police station discovered. He was promoted out of turn to the rank of head constable on Thursday because his alertness had saved an armed robbery in the house of Mr Om Prakash of Gupta Colony on September 22 this year.

So impressed were the residents of Ranbir Singh's beat in the Vijay Nagar area that they vociferously demanded the highest possible reward for the constable. The photograph shows his DCP, Mrs Kiran Bedi, and his ACP, Mr Ujjwal Misra, pinning the coveted head constable's stripes on his shoulders.

INDIAN EXPRESS
17-10-86

Drive against eve-teasing

The Hindu 22/2/87

NEW DELHI, Feb. 21.

Following the wrath of the students and staff of the Lady Irwin College against an eve-teasing incident in a DTC bus on Thursday, the North Delhi police has launched a drive against ... d 24 persons for ... the North Delhi ... said of the 24 ar- ... picking pockets ... and being in a ... nce to other pas- ... a regular feature

Crackdown on 'crime on the move'

THE STATEMAN, 22 feb, 1987

By a Staff Reporter

The "grounding" of eve-teasers and pickpockets operating in DTC buses has been started in "Mrs Bedi style" by the police in North District.

Having realized that two-thirds of the capital's population commuted by bus, the need of curbing crime in the interest of the "travelling public" assumed importance to the police, Mrs Kiran Bedi, DCP (North), said.

A week-long drive launched for the purpose ended on Saturday after 1,460 buses were checked by men in uniform leading to the "grounding" and arrest of 24 alleged pickpockets and 17 men who allegedly were teasing wo-

Cops in Mufti to check eve-teasing in varsity buses

NEW DELHI, January 20 (PTI): Policemen in Mufti will be posted in Delhi University D.T.C. ... keep the eve teasers at ba...

These policemen will ... selected D.T.C. university ... bid to apprehend eveteaser... has been taken in the w... alleged molestation of a ... last week.

Police sources said this ... in consultation with uni... college authorities here ... sources said the surprise ... these routes would be co... rotation.

सान्ध्य दैनिक वीर अर्जुन

किरन बेदी के डी.टी.सी. की 255 बसों पर छापे

कई अपराधी पकड़े गये

—कार्यालय संवाददाता—

नई दिल्ली, १६ फरवरी। उत्तरी दिल्ली में पुलिस उपायुक्त श्रीमती किरन बेदी के नेतृत्व में पुलिस ने जेब तराशों के विरुद्ध एक जबरदस्त अभियान छेड़ा है।

आपण सहज सुटून जाऊ शकतो या विचाराने, गर्दीने खचाखच भरलेल्या बसमध्ये महिला प्रवाशांची छेडाछेड करणाऱ्या पुरुषांना लगाम घालण्यासाठी 'चालत्या फिरत्या' गुन्हाला आवर घालणे हा आम्ही महिला प्रवाशांना दिलासा देण्यासाठी सुरू केलेला उपक्रम होता. आम्ही बसमध्ये अचानक तपासणी करायला सुरुवात केली. साध्या वेषातील पोलीस अचानक कोणत्याही बसमध्ये शिरून बसचे दोन्ही दरवाजे रोखून धरत. चालकाला बस रस्त्याकडेला घ्यायला सांगत आणि प्रवाशांना काही तक्रारी असतील तर त्या नोंदवण्याची विनंती करत. यामुळे गुन्ह्यांचे प्रमाण लक्षणीय कमी झाले.

शिकवण: सर्जनशील विचारसरणी व व्यावहारिक उपाययोजना यांमुळे समस्या सोडवता येते.

'OPERATION POPPY' A NEW CHAPTER IN TRIBALS LIFE
KIRAN BEDI TO SPARE NONE
I 25 KG HEROINE BEING DESTROYED IN 45 VILLAGES
CHAKRATA, May 10(HTNS)
poor people to cultivate poppy for extracting opium. However the axe is bound
opium that such a big anti poppy drive has been carried out by the Govern-
gative reports by the Himachal Times the Doordarshan and other leading Dailies. The U.P. Chief Minister had ordered a high level probe into the bunglings by two independent agencies who had reported back that what the investigative reports in the media said was true. The reports were however not made public nor was any action taken against the men actually responsible for the siphoning off of the
meant for the poor
The administrative
were completed
a few peons
level officials
never have
or opportunity
big money.
against them.
CHAKRATA HILLS TURN OPIUM HEAVEN
By P. Jain
SUN, AUG 1988

भारत हा जगातील सर्वाधिक अफू उत्पादक देशांपैकी एक आहे. भारतात अफूच्या लागवडीसाठी अधिकृत परवाना घ्यावा लागतो. पण बऱ्याच ठिकाणी त्याची बेकायदेशीर लागवड केली जाते. अशा प्रकारच्या बेकायदेशीर अफू उत्पादनातून संबंधितांना बेहिशेबी महसूलाचा स्रोत उपलब्ध होतो आणि त्यातून अगली पदार्थांच्या अवैध व्यापाराला चालना मिळते. हा प्रकार समूळ नष्ट करण्यासाठी नार्कोटिक्स कंट्रोल ब्यूरो आणि इन्टरपोल व अन्य आंतरराष्ट्रीय कायदा अंमलबजावणी संस्थांच्या संयुक्त विद्यमाने 'साफसफाई' मोहीम राबवण्यात आली.

शिकवण: तुम्ही विचारपूर्वक नियोजनबद्ध धोके पत्करल्याखेरीज आयुष्यात प्रगती करू शकत नाही.

POLICE STATION KHAWZAWL
MIZORAM

प्रत्येक आव्हान पेलण्याचा एक विशिष्ट मार्ग असतो आणि त्यावर स्थानिक संस्कृती व इतिहासाचा प्रभाव असतो. भारताच्या ईशान्य टोकाला माझी नियुक्ती झाली होती, त्या वेळी मला ही गोष्ट जाणवली. असे अडसर लोकांच्या सहभागातून दूर करता आले कारण माझ्यासारख्या, मिझोराममध्ये परक्या असलेल्या व्यक्तीपेक्षा तिथल्या लोकांना त्यावरचे उपाय माहीत होते. आम्ही सर्व संबंधित संस्था व स्थानिक लोकांना एकत्र आणून सीमेवरील अवैध व्यापाराच्या समस्येवर लक्ष एकवटले.

शिकवण: नेत्यांनी सामिलीकरण व सहयोगासाठी सदैव तयार असले पाहिजे.

जेव्हा तुम्ही पालक बनू शकता तेव्हा फक्त रक्षक बनू नका. मी दिल्लीत तुरुंग महानिरीक्षक म्हणून काम सुरू केल्यावर मी हेच केले. तिहार जेल हे जवळजवळ १०,००० कैद्यांनी खचाखच भरलेले बंदी-संस्थान होते. इथे मी सर्व कैद्यांना दिनक्रम आखून दिला, त्यामध्ये शालेय शिक्षण, व्यावसायिक कौशल्ये, आध्यात्मिक प्रवचने, क्रीडा, स्वयं-साहाय्यता अशा प्रकारचे अनेक उपक्रम सुरू केले.

शिकवण: तुमच्यावरील जबाबदारीचा थोर उद्देश लक्षात घ्या. कर्तव्यात कधीही कुचराई करू नका.

Photos: Ajay Goya

तुरुंगवास ही मानसिकदृष्ट्या फार भयंकर शिक्षा असते. ती माणसाला अध:पतनाच्या गर्तेत लोटू शकते. ही गोष्ट ओळखून आम्ही बरेच क्लेशनिवारक उपक्रम सुरू केले. त्यामध्ये आम्ही विप:श्यना ध्यान कार्यक्रम सुरू केला, ज्यायोगे कैद्यांना त्यांच्यावरील मानसिक आघाताला तोंड देण्यास साहाय्य व्हावे आणि तुरुंगातून सुटल्यावर समाजात माणूस म्हणून पूर्ववत जगता यावे. या उपक्रमाचा लाभ होतोय असे आमच्या लक्षात आले व यामुळे गुन्ह्याकडे पुन्हापुन्हा वळण्याची प्रवृत्ती कमी झाल्याचे संशोधनपर अभ्यासातूनही सिद्ध झाले आहे.

शिकवण: मानसिक सजगतेमुळे आत्मजागरूकता वृद्धिंगत होते, व ती माणसाला चुका करण्यापासून रोखते.

Better days ahead for convicts' kids born inside Tihar

by Shailendra Kumar

EXPRESS NEWS SERVICE
NEW DELHI

FOUR-YEAR-OLD ... Chandan ... not an offender, she still lives the life of ... born in the women's cell of Tihar ... ones who share her fate, and are thus ...

oker said that they have so far sent 16 children to the Kirti Nagar-based 'Home'.

What about those who were not fortunate enough to join their mothers in the jail and have nobody to look after them. Tears rolling down her cheeks Mithilesh Devi who has been an under-trial in a murder case for four years, said, "Mere do bachche hain, unko dekhane wala koi nahi hain, baap to kabhi ka mar gaya (I have two children who have nobody to look after them, their father died long back)."

... Looker said the ... ren – Ashok Kumar and Manoj Kumar ... their nights without ... ours for help they ...

Some of the kids of prisoners who were born in Tihar jail studying at the school inside the jail premises. *Express photo by R.K. Sharma.*

inted out, they ran after a caged bear shouting "Oh, such a big cat!".

In the last one year these children have been exposed to the 'out-

ent for having murdered her husband Kishan Lal. She has two kids Jitu, 10, and Deepu, 6. For a few months, Deepu has been with he...

The most happening place in town? Tihar jail, of course!*

Continuity in emergence... Courtesy: The Times of India, April 9, 1998. Caricature by Neelabh.

Artist: Shakira Scolt

अनेक अडचणी असूनही, आम्ही आशिया खंडातील सर्वात मोठ्या तुरुंगाचे सुधारगृहात रूपांतर केले. या कार्यात आम्ही या तुरुंगातील कैद्यांना सहभागी करून घेतले, तसेच शैक्षणिक व सामाजिक विकासाशी संबंधित उपक्रमांसाठी बाहेरच्या लोकांचे सहकार्य घेतले. आम्ही या तुरुंगात कैद्यांच्या मुलांसाठी 'प्लेवे स्कूल'सुद्धा सुरू केले. हा प्रकल्प इंडिया व्हिजन फाउंडेशनमार्फत आजही सुरू आहे. या संदर्भातील सर्वात उपयुक्त उपक्रम म्हणजे 'फिरती अर्ज पेटी'. या उपक्रमामुळे कैद्यांना गुप्तपणे त्यांच्या सूचना-तक्रारी देण्याची सोय उपलब्ध झाली.

शिकवण: तुम्ही कोठे आहात या गोष्टीने काही फरक पडत नाही. तुमच्या वेळाचे सुयोग्य मूल्यवर्धन करा. ही तुमची गुंतवणूक असते.

नॅशनल प्रेअर ब्रेकफास्ट मीटिंग’मध्ये राष्ट्राध्यक्ष बिल क्लिन्टन व त्यांच्या पत्नी हिलरी क्लिन्टन यांच्यासमवेत (वॉशिंग्टन डी सी, फेब्रुवारी-१९९५) (फोटो सौजन्य: आय डेअर)

डॉ. किरण बेदी यांच्या पुरस्कार स्वीकारतानाच्या भाषणातील अंश:

माननीय राष्ट्राध्यक्ष, श्रीमती मॅगसेसे, विश्वस्त आणि स्त्री-पुरुष हो, बावीस वर्षांपूर्वी मी जेव्हा श्रेष्ठ अशा भारतीय पोलीस सेवेत दाखल व्हायचे ठरवले, तेव्हा मला या सेवेत, ‘करण्याचे अधिकार’, ‘करवून घेण्याचे अधिकार’ आणि ‘सुधारण्याचे अधिकार’ असे प्रचंड सामर्थ्य दिसले. माझे ठाम मत आहे की, कोणत्याही देशातील पोलीस, मानवी हक्कांचे आणि कायद्याच्या चौकटीचे सर्वश्रेष्ठ रक्षक होऊ शकतात. रेमन मॅगसेसे पुरस्काराने माझ्याही बाबतीत काही जादुई गोष्टी केल्या आहेत.

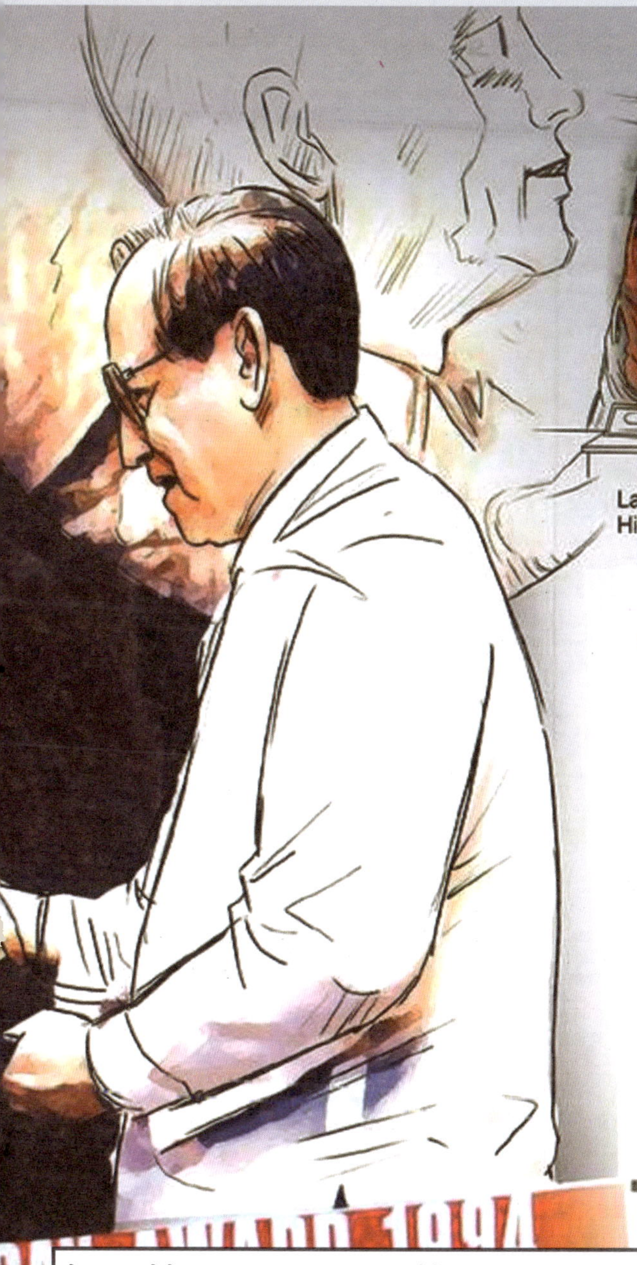

परमपूज्य दलाई लामा यांच्या हस्ते Kiran Bedi.com या संकेतस्थळाचा शुभारंभ (फोटो सौजन्य :आय डेअर)

रेमन मॅगसेसे पुरस्काराच्या मानपत्रातील अंश:

श्रीमती बेदींच्या सर्व नव्या उपक्रमांत एक विशिष्ट आकृतीबंध (पॅटर्न) दिसतो: प्रत्येक जण पोलीस व समाज यांच्यातील शत्रुत्व मोडून टाकू पाहात आहे आणि शिक्षा करणाऱ्या कठोर हातांऐवजी सर्वांनाच पुनर्वसनाचा हळुवार फुंकर घालणारा हात हवा आहे.

वयाच्या पंचेचाळिसाव्या वर्षीसुद्धा श्रीमती बेदी यांच्याजवळ तारुण्यातला उत्साह, शिस्त, आत्मविश्वास आणि स्पर्धात्मक वृत्ती टिकून आहे. यंत्रणा झुगारण्यास त्या आतूर आहेत. त्या म्हणतात, ''प्रवाहाविरुद्ध पोहणे फार कठीण असते, पण किमान जिथे कोणीही पोहोचू शकत नाही अशा ठिकाणी तुम्ही पोहोचता.''

१९९४ सालच्या, सरकारी सेवेसाठी दिल्या जाणाऱ्या रेमन मॅगसेसे पुरस्कारासाठी श्रीमती किरण बेदी यांची निवड करताना विश्वस्त मंडळाला, श्रीमती बेदी यांनी भारतातील पोलिसांमध्ये आपल्या चैतन्यपूर्ण नेतृत्वाने जो आत्मविश्वास निर्माण केला आणि गुन्हेगारी रोखण्यासाठी, व्यसनग्रस्तांच्या पुनर्वसनासाठी आणि मानवतापूर्ण तुरुंग सुधारणांसाठी जे प्रभावी अभिनव उपक्रम सुरू केले, ते प्रशंसनीय व दखल घेण्याजोगे वाटतात.

रेमन मॅगसेसे पुरस्कार हा आशियातील नोबेल पुरस्कार मानला जातो. हा पुरस्कार म्हणजे, पोलिसांचे काम केवळ अटक करणे व तपास लावणे इथवरच नसून अपराध रोखणे व गुन्हेगारांना सुधारणे हेही असते, या धारणेला मिळालेली आंतरराष्ट्रीय मान्यता होती. पोलीस जेव्हा लोकांची मने जिंकतात, त्यांच्या हृदयात स्थान मिळवतात आणि त्यांचा विश्वासही जिंकतात तेव्हा ते त्यांचे कर्तव्य सर्वोत्तम रितीने पार पाडतात असे म्हणता येईल. हा पुरस्कार ही 'थ्री-सी मॉडेल'ला मिळालेली मान्यता होती. थ्री-सी-मॉडेल म्हणजे collective, corrective आणि community policing.

सामूहिक, सुधारात्मक व सामुदायिक या त्रिसूत्रीवर आधारलेल्या या 'मॉडेल'ला आंतरराष्ट्रीय स्तरावर पसंतीची पावती मिळाली.

शिकवण: तुम्ही जे कार्य निवडले असेल त्यासाठी सर्वशक्तीनिशी प्रयत्न करा. तुमचे कार्यच बोलेल.

Cops on their toes from today, Kiran Bedi is here

Computerisation of police stations, check on traffic violations, welfare of forces' kin among priorities

IGP invites NGOs to meet SHOs

EXPRESS NEWS SERVICE
CHANDIGARH, APRIL 17

INSPECTOR General of Police Dr Kiran Bedi has invited representatives of city-based NGOs to a meeting on May 1, where they would be introduced to the area SHOs to have smoother interaction between the two.

The IGP was participating in a discussion on "Empowerment of Women", organised by the local chapter of Indian Council of Social

Thanks to Kiran Bedi, cops get a weekly off

EXPRESS NEWS SERVICE
CHANDIGARH, APRIL 25

FOR the first time in the 33-year-old history of the Chandi-

माझे उच्चशिक्षण चंदीगड या शहरात झाले. मी तिथे पोलीस महानिरीक्षक पदावर नियुक्त झाले. मी तिथे पहिल्या दिवसापासूनच, माझ्या सर्व क्षेत्रांतील अनुभवाच्या आधारे काम सुरू केले... पोलीस ठाण्यांना दररोज आकस्मिक भेटी, बीट ऑफिसर्सच्या नियुक्त्या, महिला पोलिसांच्या 'फील्ड'वर नियुक्त्या, वाहतूक नियमांची काटेकोर अंमलबजावणी, बिगर सरकारी संस्थांचा सहभाग, 'डे केअर सेंटर' व आठवडी सुट्टी याद्वारे कर्मचाऱ्यांच्या हिताचा विचार अशा अनेक गोष्टी सुरू केल्या. आम्ही काही आठवड्यांतच शहराचे रूप पालटून टाकले आणि लोकांनाही हे सगळे खूप आवडले.

शिकवण: तुमच्या टीमसोबत झपाट्याने कामाला लागा.

LG ACTIVATES A BETTER DELHI CAMPAIGN, KIRAN BEDI IN TOW

Kamaljeet Singh TIMES OF INDIA, 15 APR 1997

received in a day, a sample of at least 25 of them are sent for a "test check", a new method adopted by Bedi. In the "test check" method, an inspector visits the field and prepares a feedback note based on the statements of both the complainant and the concerned authority. If the statements of both parties vary, the inspector's report is then referred to higher authorities. "In this process, we are not only responding to a complaint immediately, but also ensure that field

DELHI TIMES, THE TIMES OF INDIA 21 APR 1998

Capital Life

The new Lt Governor's legacy: Task forces, 600 wardens and a 24-hour control room

Upasna Trakroo

As the new Lt Governor assumes charge, he faces the task of deciding the fate of several task

various task forces and other schemes of his predecessor. "I would like to study these task forces and the citizen warden scheme and then I will decide what steps to initiate.

The Delhi renewal task force, consisting of environment management wing and vehicular pollution section, was also created. The department of urban development was

kicked off quite a controversy with the municipal counsellors who were up in arms over what they thought was "unconstitutional" encroachment into their role.

initiated by the former LG has been that of the citizen warden scheme. Ordinary people have been able to resolve a large number of their problems by themselves," says Dr Bedi.

मी दिल्लीचे नायब राज्यपाल तेजेंद्र खन्ना यांची विशेष सचिव म्हणून काम करत असताना, आम्ही त्यांचे कार्यालय लोकांसाठी खऱ्या अर्थाने खुले केले. लोकांना तिथे प्रवेश सहज उपलब्ध होऊ लागला. 'सिटिझन वॉर्डन स्कीम्स' सारख्या अनेक उपक्रमांबरोबरच आम्ही तक्रार निवारणासाठी २४ तास कंट्रोल रूम सुरू केली. या उपक्रमाद्वारे सर्व तक्रारींची योग्य दखल घेतली जात असे आणि तक्रारदाराचे समाधान होत आहे का यावरही लक्ष दिले जात असे. यामुळे शहराच्या व्यवस्थापनात चैतन्य आले. नायब राज्यपाल भवन त्या वेळपर्यंत सामान्यांसाठी इतके खुले कधीच नव्हते.

शिकवण: पद जितके उत्तुंग, तितके ते लोकांना सहज पोहोचण्याच्या आवाक्यात असले पाहिजे.

Police taught meditatio

By Our Staff Reporter

NEW DELHI, Jan 12.

Before the police personnel "police" others, it
s important that they learn to police them-
selves. No ...

to master themselves

ow to serve society. The best service to God is to
erve society for the betterment of people with-
ut any personal benefit."

Another official who underwent the course,
... says, " the Vipassana shivir
... on a spiritual and mental
... of mental purification
... course is a foundation
... living a meaningful.

... pe for revival of the
... ana." Ms. Bedi says
... posted to the Police
... alan, six months
... low morale of the
Vipassana for all
... " she avers.
... the Vipassa-
... the

दिल्ली पोलीस ट्रेनिंग कॉलेजमध्ये आम्ही प्रत्येक उमेदवाराला आगामी काही दशकांसाठी सुसज्ज करत होतो. प्रत्येक उमेदवार बौद्धिक, भावनिक व आध्यात्मिक कौशल्य निपुण होणे आवश्यक असल्यामुळे आम्ही सर्व जण दहा दिवसांच्या विप:श्यना ध्यान शिबिराला हजर राहिलो. या ध्यानधारणाने आम्हाला पोलीस सेवा बजावत इतरांना शिस्त लावतानाच स्वत:ला शिस्त लावण्याचे व आत्मसंयमनाचे धडे शिकवले. या प्रशिक्षणादरम्यान, उमेदवारांना अत्यंत खडतर शारीरिक प्रशिक्षणाबरोबरच अत्यंत आवश्यक असलेल्या इतर कौशल्याचे (सॉफ्ट स्किल्स) प्रशिक्षण देण्यात आले.

शिकवण: 'मन' व 'हात' या प्रशिक्षणाविना, फक्त 'डोक्या'पुरत्या सीमित असलेल्या प्रशिक्षणाचा परिणामकारक उपयोग होत नाही.

'ब्यूरो ऑफ पोलीस रिसर्च ॲन्ड डेव्हलपमेंट' ही भारतातील पोलीस प्रशिक्षण व संशोधनाची दिशादर्शक संस्था आहे. या संस्थेचे नेतृत्व अधिकारी करतात. पण इथे साधनस्त्रोतांची अत्यंत कमतरता होती. इथेही आम्ही आधीच्यासारखीच सिव्हिल सोसायटीची मदत घेतली आणि संशोधनासंदर्भात विद्यापीठाच्या कुलसचिवांना निमंत्रित केले. या कार्याला गती देण्यासाठी, दररोज सकाळी दहा वाजता योजना व आढावा बैठक घेण्यात येत असे. यामुळे बहुतेकसे अधिकारी या योजनांच्या अंमलबजावणीवर लक्ष केंद्रित करू लागले.

शिकवण: मीटिंगमध्ये मुख्य मुद्यावर लक्ष केंद्रित करा, सामूहिक ऊर्जेचा वापर करून घ्या आणि आवश्यकतेनुसार, कमीत कमी मीटिंग्ज घ्या.

हे अशा प्रकारचे काम होते, जिथे 'स्काय इज द लिमिट' म्हणतात तसा आवाका होता. आपत्ती व्यवस्थापनासाठी सज्जता करण्याच्या कामात, 'सिव्हिल डिफेन्स'च्या परिघात संपूर्ण दिल्लीचा समावेश होता. आम्ही यासंदर्भात 'यलो अ‍ॅलर्ट' ही संकल्पना साकार केली होती - याचा अर्थ असा की, कोणत्याही आपत्तीमध्ये सर्व प्रशिक्षित सिव्हिल डिफेन्स/होमगार्ड स्वयंसेवकांना सज्ज होण्याचा सामूहिक संदेश मिळेल.

शिकवण: तुम्ही कोणत्याही क्षेत्रात काम करत असलात, तरी तुमच्या कार्याचा खरा उद्देश लक्षात घ्या. कोणतेही काम लहान अथवा मोठे नसते.

संयुक्त राष्ट्रसंघांच्या सेक्रेटरी जनरल यांची सिव्हिलियन पोलीस अॅडव्हायजर म्हणून नेमणूक होणारी पहिली महिला बनण्याचा मान मला लाभला. संयुक्त राष्ट्रसंघांच्या शांतता स्थापना कार्य विभागाच्या संचालकपदी काम करताना मला आंतरराष्ट्रीय स्तरावर काम करता आले. आमच्या पोलीस विभागाने आफ्रिका, आशिया व युरोपमध्ये सोळा शांतता स्थापना-मोहिमांत सेवा बजावली. आम्ही युद्धग्रस्त देशांसह अन्य ठिकाणी शांतता व सुव्यवस्था पुनर्स्थापित करण्यासाठी प्रयत्न केले.

शिकवण: आंतरराष्ट्रीय पटाची ओळख आणि सांस्कृतिक विभिन्नता माणसाची विचारप्रक्रिया समृद्ध करते व त्याची वैचारिक कुवत वाढवते.

नेतृत्वाचे पारंपरिक मॉडेल

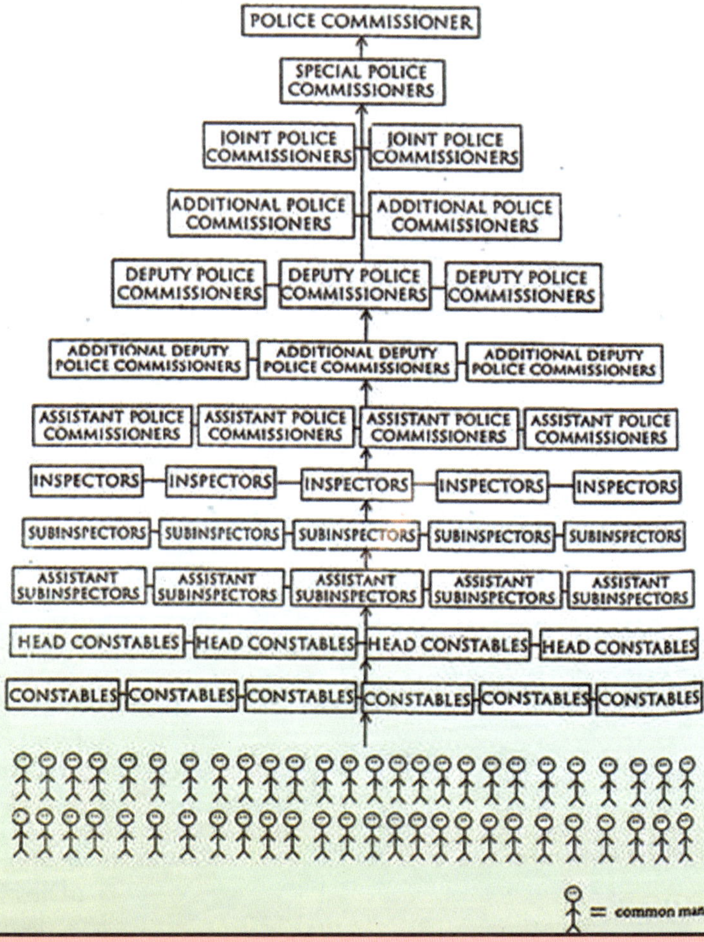

- या मॉडेलमधील नेतृत्व, आदेश व नियंत्रण याद्वारे काम करते
- हा अत्यंत केंद्रित व इतर सहकाऱ्यांपासून नेतृत्वाला दूर करणारा प्रकार आहे.
- हे नेतृत्व आपले पद व पदाची ताकद याद्वारे काम करवून घेते.
- या मॉडेलमुळे समस्या चिघळतात व लांबणीवर टाकल्या जातात.
- हे मॉडेल असंवेदनशील, पैशासाठी काम करणारे, शिक्षा करणारे व संशयावर चालणारे असते.
- हे मॉडेल लोकांच्या मनात भय निर्माण करून आपला वचक बसवते.
- हे मॉडेल लिंगभेदाच्या बाबतीत असंवेदनशील आहे आणि कधीकधी आपल्या मर्जीतील माणसांची नेमणूक वा हकालपट्टी करते.
- या मॉडेलमुळे विश्वासार्ह प्रतिक्रिया मिळण्याजोगी यंत्रणा निर्माण होत नाही, कारण इथे हांजी हांजी करणाऱ्या खुशमस्कऱ्यांची व कंपूशाहीची चलती असते.
- हे मॉडेल कधीकधी घाबरतेसुद्धा, पण निडरपणाचा आव आणते.
- हे मॉडेल परिस्थिती कायम 'जैसे थे' राखते, कारण परिवर्तन धोक्याचे वाटते.
- या मॉडेलमुळे भविष्यात नकारात्मक नेतृत्व निर्माण होते आणि चुकीचे आदर्श घालून देते.
- हे मॉडेल फलनिष्पत्ती घडवू शकते, पण त्याची इतरांना किंमत मोजायला लावून.

नेतृत्वाचे सर्जनशील मॉडेल

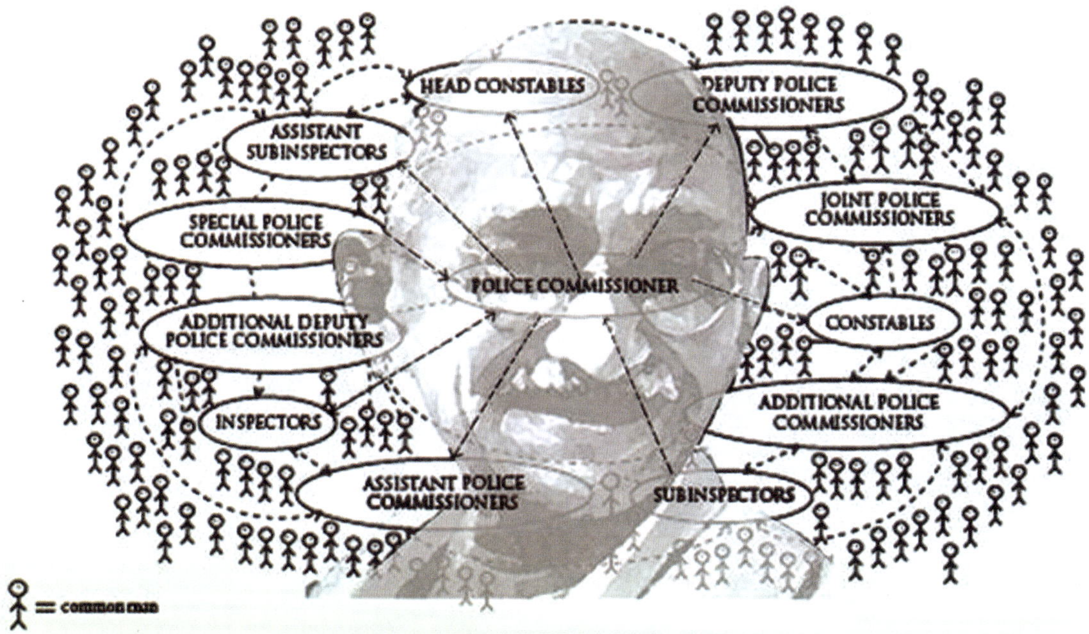

- ही मुख्यत्वे, कार्याची गतीशील व सर्वसमावेशक पद्धत आहे.
- हे मॉडेल सक्रिय व रचनात्मक कार्य घडवते व सर्जनशील मार्ग दाखवते.
- हे मॉडेल परिणामकारक फलनिष्पत्तीचा पाठपुरावा करते, तसेच हे मॉडेल आत्म-सुधारणा घडवते.
- या मॉडेलमधील नेतृत्वासाठी कोणतेही पद (रॅन्क) वरिष्ठ अथवा कनिष्ठ नसते, कारण या मॉडेलमध्ये 'माणूस' हीच अनमोल ऊर्जा मानली जाते त्यामुळे तिचा आदर केला जातो व ती एकवटली जाते.
- या मॉडेलमध्ये लोकांची क्षमतांनुसार नेमणूक केली जाते आणि मग त्यांचा भविष्याच्या दृष्टीने विकास केला जातो.
- या मॉडेलमधील नेतृत्व न मळलेल्या वाटा निवडते आणि नवनव्या कल्पनांना जन्म देते.
- हे मॉडेल संपर्काची सर्व माध्यमे खुली ठेवते आणि ऐकीव गोष्टींवर अवलंबून राहात नाही.
- या मॉडेलमधील नेतृत्व इतरांना श्रेय देताना, दोष स्वत:कडे घेते.
- या नेतृत्वाचे उत्तम लक्षण म्हणजे आपल्या संस्थेला काळाच्या पुढे राहाण्यासाठी सर्जनशील विचार देणे.

या मालिकेतील पुढील पुस्तकातून...

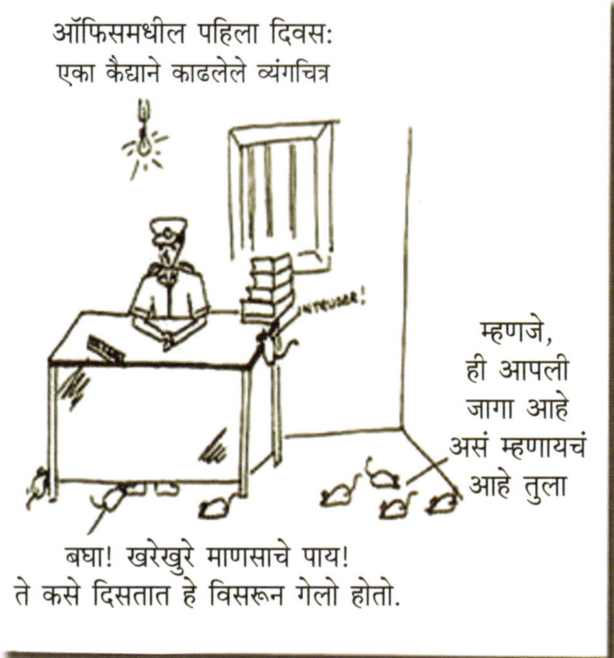

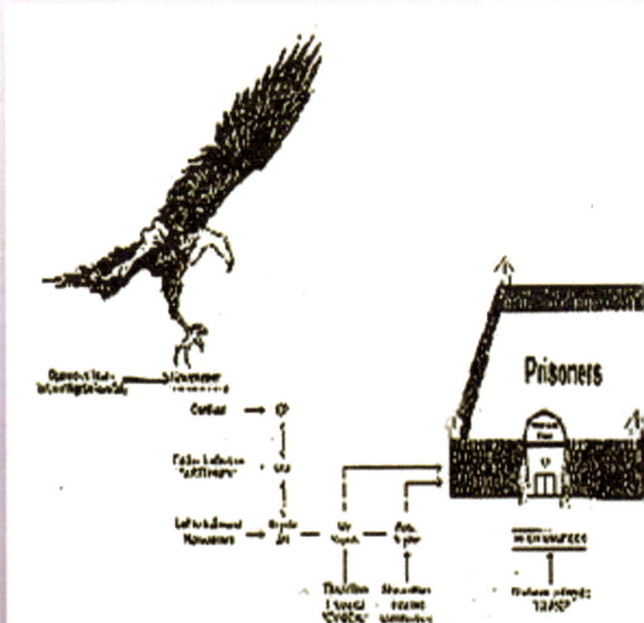

Source: It's Always Pos

कृतज्ञता

Photo: Ajay Goyal

माझ्या 'टॉप कॉप' कार्यकालातील हे सचित्र दर्शन यांच्याविना शक्य झाले नसते

- माझे डॅडी, त्यांनी मला सगळ्या व्यक्तिगत नोंदीसह कागदपत्रे व्यवस्थित सांभाळून ठेवण्याचे मोल शिकवले.
- माझे कुटुंब, इंडिया व्हिजन फाउंडेशन आणि माझा खासगी स्टाफ - त्यांनी गेली कित्येक दशके मला दफ्तरखाना व्यवस्थित ठेवायला मदत केली आहे.
- प्रसारमाध्यमात घटनांचे वार्तांकन करणारे सर्व जण त्यांनी त्या-त्या वेळी त्यांच्या कामाचा भाग म्हणून हे केले असेल. पण ते आता माझ्या दफ्तरखान्याचा भाग बनले आहे.
- डायमंड पब्लिशर्सचे प्रकाशक श्री. नरेंदर कुमार वर्मा. भावी पिढ्यांसाठी अशा प्रकारचे पुस्तक प्रकाशित करणे ही त्यांचीच कल्पना आहे. 'मेकिंग ऑफ दी कॉप' नंतरचे हे दुसरे पुस्तक आहे.
- या मालिकेच्या संपादिका त्यांनी माझ्या संपूर्ण संग्रहातून युवावर्गाला उत्सुकता वाटू शकेल, शिवाय सर्जनशील नेतृत्वासाठी आवश्यक अशा घटना निवडण्यासाठी खूप परिश्रमपूर्वक साहाय्य केले आहे.
- चित्रकार श्री. प्रभात श्रीवास्तव यांच्या रेखाटनांनी या चित्रदर्शनाला जिवंत स्पर्श घडवला आहे.
- दिल्ली पोलीस, मिझोराम, गोवा, चंडीगढ तिहार कारागृह (कैद्यांसह), होम गार्डस् व सिव्हिल डिफेन्स संचलनालय, ब्यूरो ऑफ पोलीस रिसर्च अॅन्ड डेव्हलपमेंट, भारत सरकार, नार्कोटिक्स कंट्रोल ब्यूरो, संयुक्त राष्ट्रसंघ, नायब राज्यपाल, दिल्ली यांचे कार्यालय, रेमन मॅगसेसे फाउंडेशनमधील सर्व व्यक्ती.

- ना-नफा तत्त्वावरील संस्था, कंपन्या, व्यावसायिक व्यक्ती, स्वयंसेवक आणि विद्यार्थी - हे सर्व जण 'कम्युनिटी पोलिसिंग' व तुरुंग सुधारणा कार्याचा अविभाज्य घटक राहिले आहेत.
- आणि माझे पोलीस सेवेतील, प्रशासकीय सेवेतील, तसेच राजकीय प्रशासनातील वरिष्ठ.... मी परिवर्तनाला चालना देत असताना ते माझ्या सोबत राहिले होते.

या पुस्तकाद्वारे होणाऱ्या कमाईची रक्कम इंडिया व्हिजन फाउंडेशन संचलित डॉ. रीटा पेशावरिया मेनन फेलोशिप फंडात जमा केली जाईल.